THEN & NOW

FORT COLLINS

OPPOSITE: For many decades, Fort Collins was an agricultural town. It certainly was around 1900, when this photograph of Plattner Implement Company was taken. Located on the west side of Linden Street, Plattner's sold and repaired harvesters, mowers, cultivators, and hay tools and advertised the "finest buggies and wagons that ever came to Fort Collins." The business was run from Denver by five Plattner brothers and one sister; one owner, George Plattner, stands in the doorway. (Fort Collins Museum Local History Archive, H00766, *c.* 1900.)

THEN & NOW

FORT COLLINS

Barbara Fleming
and Malcolm McNeill

*This book is dedicated to the preservationists, past, present, and future,
who work to protect the historical buildings of Fort Collins that we all enjoy.*

ON THE FRONT COVER: Although it now stands empty, 210 Linden Street once housed Carl Lauterbach's cigar factory. Taken in 1887, this photograph shows Lauterbach and his wife, Catherine, standing center left. Next door (left) is the establishment of A. McDougall, merchant tailor. Since the departure of the cigar factory, the building has seen varied uses, but its appearance has changed little. (Fort Collins Museum Local History Archive, H01469, 1887.)

ON THE BACK COVER: Featuring a two-story center section, this handsome passenger depot on Laporte Avenue, east of Mason Street, was built in 1889 by the Colorado and Southern Railroad and is shown in this 1912 photograph with Oldsmobile railroad cars on the track in front of the depot. A modification of Oldsmobile's popular curved-dash automobile, these are probably being used by railroad executives on an inspection trip. (Fort Collins Museum Local History Archive, H00258, 1912.)

CONTENTS

ACKNOWLEDGMENTS

We gratefully acknowledge the cooperation and assistance of the Fort Collins Museum Local History Archive and the use of vintage images from its extensive photographic collection. Lesley Drayton, archivist, and Pat Walker, research assistant, gave us invaluable aid in our research.

We thank Arlene Ahlbrandt and Nadine Gates, who provided vintage photographs along with memories of an earlier time in Fort Collins; Hazel Graves, who shared postcard images; and Carol Tunner, Wayne Sundberg, and Arthur Mitchell, who provided help in researching some of the more obscure photograph locations.

At the end of each caption we have included the source, and when known, the approximate date of the vintage photograph. Many of the images in this book appear courtesy of the Fort Collins Museum Local History Archive (FCM) and from the personal collection of Malcolm McNeill (MEM). A few images have been provided from other personal collections, and they are specifically credited as they appear in the book. The images from the Fort Collins Museum also include an image number that should be used when making inquiries. All of the modern photographs are courtesy of author and photographer Malcolm McNeill.

Introduction

With the advent of Native American uprisings, the United States established an outpost on the banks of the Cache la Poudre River on the high plains of northeastern Colorado on July 22, 1862. Fanning out from the fort, cavalry troops patrolled the area vigorously until June 9, 1864, when the river overflowed, inundating the camp. The commander ordered the camp relocated a few miles downstream on higher ground.

The new fort was abandoned in 1867. Rather than being the end of the story, this was the beginning. Settlers began coming to the verdant, fertile river valley. By 1872, a new town, the Agricultural Colony, had been established. One year later, this new town was platted and incorporated as Fort Collins.

Despite droughts, grasshopper invasions, bank failures, and other setbacks, the little town grew steadily. Two factors favored growth—the establishment of a land-grant college in the early 1870s and the arrival of the railroad in 1877. Fort Collins was on its way.

By the beginning of the 20th century, the population was nearly 3,000. Agriculture was the mainstay of the town. Wooden structures, repeatedly decimated by fires, had been replaced by brick and stone buildings. Downtown took on a unique, picturesque character.

Fort Collins went through many years when historic preservation was not a priority; buildings historians would now cherish were lost. But downtown—now labeled Old Town as the new town grew up around it—retained its architectural integrity and beauty; so much so, in fact, that Walt Disney used it as a model for Main Street in Disneyland.

We published an earlier book in Arcadia Publishing's Images of America series entitled *Fort Collins: The Miller Photographs*. With that book, we showed Fort Collins through the eyes of Mark Miller, a local photographer who worked in the city for 60 years. With this book, we can go further back in time, selecting vintage photographs that show readers what Fort Collins looked like a century ago. Just as importantly, the side-by-side comparisons of the vintage photographs with what the buildings or locations look like today document changes the city has seen. These comparisons can be revealing, thrilling, or depressing but are, we hope, always interesting.

In presenting this overview of old Fort Collins, we chose to begin with a chapter on railroads because the arrival of the railroad was so vital to the survival and growth of the town. From the time the first trains came in 1877, the future of Fort Collins seemed assured. Farmers and ranchers could get their goods to market, and the town would not be bypassed by progress. But the arrival of the railroads left some marks, especially the return of the Union Pacific Railroad (UP) to Fort Collins in 1910. Forced into receivership during the financial panic of 1893, the UP had to sell its subsidiary railroad that served Fort Collins. When times improved, the UP approached the town fathers with a plan to return, a plan that required acquiring property along some of the most developed streets in the city. More than 100 structures were torn down to make way for the UP's tracks and depots. Fort Collins gained a second railroad but lost some of the most historic buildings in the city. Readers will see some of the results in the railroad and hotel chapters.

From there we move to commercial establishments in chapter two. The businesses we chose emerged and thrived thanks to the growth of the town. It should be noted here that in the town's early days, a building that housed multiple businesses was referred to as a "block," a usage different from the contemporary understanding of a section from one intersection to the next. Thus, when we refer to, for example, the Trimble Block, it is a single building.

Our third chapter looks at the hotels that served customers who came by rail, many of which disappeared or deteriorated as the automobile gained popularity, although one hotel, the Armstrong, was built in the 1920s to serve automobile travelers. However, in the 1880s and 1890s, while the horse was still king, hotels vied to be as close as possible to the depots and to get passengers to their establishments quickly and conveniently.

At one time, downtown Fort Collins was dotted with churches. Our next chapter presents some of these beautiful structures, few of which survived the gradual evolution of downtown, particularly College Avenue, into a business rather than a residential district. Fortunately, a small number of these churches remain in the Old Town area, and most of them are still used for worship.

The area now known as Old Town, bounded loosely by Riverside Drive and Lemay Avenue to the east, Shields Street to the west, the Poudre River to the north, and Prospect Street to the south, also included several schools. We devote a chapter to these buildings, most of which are gone. As the town grew south and west, new schools went up in the new neighborhoods, supplanting the earliest schools. One of the first community efforts in the small frontier town was the establishment of a public grammar school. By the beginning of the 20th century, a high school had been added. No book on Fort Collins would be complete without mentioning Colorado State University, and we have included some images from the campus.

The last chapter includes many municipal buildings and structures that supported the community in a variety of ways: to house fire engines, to hold county records and a jail, to accommodate the National Guard, and to treat the sick, for example. Along with its educational system, Fort Collins was a progressive town, with hospitals, a public reading room, and a streetcar line in place by the early years of the 20th century. Until it ended in 1951, Fort Collins was the smallest city in the country to have a streetcar system.

Then and Now photography can be a challenge when a building is gone. Sometimes, in trying to identify exactly where a building stood, the best we could do was make an educated guess after consulting early maps and knowledgeable local historians. In these cases, we have come as close as we could to placing the modern image in the same spot and from the same angle.

The images we chose were done so after finding a photograph of a vintage building that we really liked and that had a story we wanted to tell rather than presenting a particular point of view about historic preservation in Fort Collins. Today our town has become a city, with a population of around 130,000, and historic preservation is a high priority. The city, along with several organizations, works hard to retain and sustain historic structures. It is a good time for historic preservation in our city.

We hope you enjoy this look back at Fort Collins and the changes that occurred during the past century. We give you Fort Collins around 1900 and Fort Collins around 2010.

THE RAILROADS

Colorado Central brought the railroad to Fort Collins in 1877. With it came Fort Collins's first railroad depot, an all-purpose station for passengers, freight, and the railroad agent. The building, on the west side of Mason Street, north of Laporte Avenue, was razed in 1906 and replaced by a brick freight house and a separate new passenger depot on the east side of the street. C. E. Congore, the station agent, stands second from right. (FCM H02001, *c.* 1892.)

The Colorado and Southern Railroad passenger depot on Laporte Avenue at Mason Street was built in 1889 and served Fort Collins for more than 60 years. By 1952, rail passenger service had given way to the automobile and the stone depot, which projected into Laporte Avenue and had to be razed to improve the flow of traffic. (FCM H00258, *c.* 1912.)

The Colorado and Southern engine house was built in 1908 to shelter steam engines. It was probably located north of Cherry Street at Meldrum Street, where the houses are shown in the modern image. Initially it was three bays wide; in 1929, a motor car (a self-propelled passenger car) stall was added to the north side of the structure. Later used for automobile storage, it sat vacant until 1981, when it was razed. (FCM H07745.)

"Poor, indeed, is the man who could not afford . . . at least a residence today," lamented the *Weekly Courier* newspaper on January 27, 1910, as Union Pacific auctioned off properties it had purchased to make way for railroad tracks. Most buildings were sold for the materials. With little sense of history the rest were demolished, including the elegant Tedmon House hotel. Jefferson Street today bears little resemblance to the dirt roads along which the auctioneers moved by wagon from building to building. (FCM H01610, 1910.)

The Old Grout Stage Barn, at the northwest corner of Pine and Jefferson Streets, was the first livery stable in Fort Collins. At the time of the 1910 UP auction, it was sold for the hand-hewn logs that framed it. A new passenger depot would take its place. (FCM H06626, *c.* 1870.)

Among the more than 100 buildings that were auctioned off were these two at the northeast corner of Linden and Jefferson Streets, the W.A. Collins Secondhand Store and the Fort Collins Buggy Company, which once boasted of having sold enough buggies to fill several miles if lined end to end. The Collins Store once belonged to W. C. Stover and was the first commercial building constructed with bricks in Fort Collins. Today the Open Door Mission has replaced these structures. (FCM H00926, *c.* 1907.)

With its auction completed, the railroad was ready to begin work on the tracks—until John Hoffman, who owned a flour mill right next to the tracks on Riverside Drive between Myrtle and Mulberry Streets, raised legal objections that held up proceedings for nearly a year. The railroad finally settled with Hoffman and was able to complete laying tracks. The small feed mill shown above, built in 1894, had been joined by a larger flour mill before the confrontation took place. (FCM H02392, *c.* 1894.)

After the Union Pacific Railroad bought about $400,000 worth of properties along Jefferson Street and Riverside Drive to install a passenger railroad track, UP built this colorful passenger depot on the north side of Jefferson Street at Pine Street, which still stands. It currently houses a restaurant. (FCM H06180, 1928.)

THE RAILROADS

THE COMMERCIAL BUILDINGS

Even when Fort Collins was still a small frontier town, businesses appeared to meet locals' needs. Some accommodated a variety of needs, like this shoe store/bicycle repair shop located at Walnut and Pine Streets. As the town grew, larger, more specialized commercial establishments came along. (FCM H01530, c. 1890.)

When Fort Collins was in its early years, the horse was the primary means of getting around. Nothing could be more important to a businessman or homeowner than a livery stable to house the animals. Like other businesses associated with the horse, the Earnest and Branner Livery Stable, 127–129 East Mountain Avenue, disappeared when the automobile rendered horse-powered transportation obsolete. Perhaps symbolically, the building has been replaced by a parking lot. (FCM H01521, *c*.1882.)

Along with stables, the blacksmith filled a critical function in the horse-and-buggy days. Although there are still blacksmiths today, just as there are still horses, businesses like Jerry's Blacksmith Shop, located at 232 Jefferson Street, were supplanted by auto repair shops as the automobile gained in popularity. It seems likely that the elk's head with horseshoes is gone forever. (FCM H01508, *c.* 1890.)

Also serving the noble beast, Hay and Grain (destroyed by fire in 1889) was located at the northeast corner of Jefferson and Pine Streets and belonged to Billy Patterson, a good friend of Buffalo Bill Cody. A pioneer settler, Patterson was variously a Native American fighter and a freighter, a county clerk, a businessman, and a town favorite famed for his practical jokes. After his death, Cody visited Fort Collins and was instrumental in memorializing Patterson, who had donated land for the new agricultural college years before. A plaque near Spruce Hall commemorates all the donors. (FCM H02790, *c*. 1885.)

Davis Carpenter and Contractor, at 140 South College Avenue, was one of many thriving businesses on College Avenue in 1897. Note the false front on the building. False fronts were popular on commercial buildings in the West in the last half of the 19th century as a way to add an air of dignity to a hastily constructed building. By 1910, the original structure had been razed, and two newer buildings had taken its place. (FCM H02850.)

The Miller Block, at the southeast corner of Linden and Walnut Streets, is a survivor from the 1880s, outlasting years of devastating downtown fires followed by years of heedless progress. Frank C. Miller constructed this building in 1888 and added to it in 1891. Until local prohibition in 1896, Miller sold liquor; his store featured a private sampling room. With D. F. Armitage, Miller operated the Fair Store after prohibition. (Above, FCM H02014, *c.* 1890; Below, MEM, *c.* 1910.)

THE COMMERCIAL BUILDINGS

In January, 1910, the buggy building (above) was part of a Union Pacific Railroad auction of buildings on land the railroad had bought. Platform wagons carried auctioneers from building to building as the UP sold over 150 structures, one for only ten dollars. Some were moved, others demolished. The Union Pacific Passenger Depot, 200 Jefferson Street, replaced some of the auctioned buildings. Here it is decked out for the 1928 July Fourth celebration. (FCM H06180).

One of the first settlers in Fort Collins was Peter Anderson, whose early pioneering years were decidedly colorful. A farmer, freighter, stockman, cattleman, bank director, and merchant, Anderson (center) opened this mercantile at 222 Walnut Street in 1888 next to a cigar factory. Anderson prospered, becoming a prominent local citizen. Andersonville, near the sugar beet factory, was once his sheep-feeding farm. Today these buildings, still standing, are part of Old Town's retail and restaurant district. (FCM H00863, *c.* 1906.)

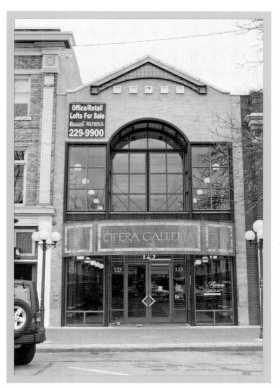

Davy Groceries on North College Avenue, one of many small, family-owned stores scattered throughout the town, was serving Fort Collins residents as early as 1883. Like grocery stores today, though on a smaller scale, these stores provided a wide variety of merchandise. Captain Davy, as Thomas H. Davy was locally known, advertised imported chocolate and cocoa, improved hygienic new-era coffee, and "Sussex horse radish flour to make bone, nerve, muscle and a kind disposition." Today the Opera Galleria has taken the place of this little store. (FCM H02771, *c.* 1880.)

Violet Flower (left) operated this hat shop at 125 West Mountain Avenue (then called Mountain View Avenue) in the early 1900s. She is shown here with Mable Rogers, possibly a helper in the shop. At this time, etiquette demanded that a lady wear a hat when she went out. Millinery shops like Flower's served this need. Today the site is occupied by a locally owned ice cream shop. (FCM H05265, c. 1910.)

Friedberg's Dry Goods Store, in business until the mid-1930s, was at 161 Linden Street. Now demolished, it has been replaced by a newer building housing a card shop. Dry-goods stores sold all manner of merchandise, including clothing, fabrics, notions, and all the latest in small appliances. Though the Jewish population in Fort Collins was small, its members were active in the community. (FCM H06186, *c.* 1927.)

According to an 1889 *Fort Collins Courier* article, Frank Stover was the pioneer druggist of Fort Collins, in business as early as 1874. The photograph of this store on the southwest corner of Linden and Jefferson Streets shows the front of his new one-story business, opened in 1888. The article described it as "very handsomely fitted up," with "an elegant Taft soda water fountain where many and varied flavors attract thirsty groups." (FCM H01432, *c.* 1900.)

By late 1905, Stover needed more room, and a second floor was added to his drugstore. The angled, glass storefront was a casualty of the expansion. This photograph of a parade at Linden and Jefferson Streets was taken during Fort Collins's Semi-Centennial celebration. The two-story Stover's drugstore is in the background. The building now houses a store selling earth-friendly goods. (FCM H00768, c. 1914.)

A. W. Scott was another early druggist in Fort Collins, where competition between drugstores was keen. Scott took the lead when he installed a nickel phonograph in 1891. In 1907, Scott pleaded guilty to selling liquor beyond his quota, but the charge and fine did not hurt his business. The Scott Drugstore occupied several sites, eventually arriving at this location in the 100 block of South College Avenue, which is now a restaurant and commercial space. (FCM H22309, *c.* 1931.)

THE COMMERCIAL BUILDINGS

Owl was another early Fort Collins drugstore, shown here in Franklin Avery's stone structure at the northeast corner of Mountain and College Avenues. The building was constructed in 1897 and was first used as the home of the First National Bank. This image can be dated to around 1908 by the dirt streets, early automobiles, and the Denver and Interurban trolley car. The view is of one of the most important commercial blocks in Fort Collins. Today various businesses and offices occupy the building. (MEM, *c.* 1908.)

A. C. Kissock, best known as the "father of Fort Collins's sewer system," had this building designed for his business by Fort Collins's premier architect, Montezuma Fuller. Destroyed by a fire in 1895, it was rebuilt and housed a number of businesses and organizations. This photograph shows Bock Furniture and its delivery wagons, an early location for Scott's Drugs, and the Odd Fellows Lodge on the second floor. On the National Register of Historic Places, the building at 117–121 East Mountain Avenue is still home to retail stores. (FCM H02471, *c.*1905.)

THE COMMERCIAL BUILDINGS

Ed Trimble and his brother Robert, sons of pioneer William Trimble, built this block in 1903. Note the group of men standing on the balcony over the doorway. Businesses in these buildings in the 100 block of North College Avenue included a billiard parlor, a ladies' furnishings store, a restaurant in Trimble Court (around the corner), and a bicycle shop. Still standing today, the buildings are used for retail businesses. Trimble Court houses an artisans' cooperative. (FCM H00187, *c.* 1904.)

In 1905, Irishman John Whitton constructed this building for his company called J. Whitton and Company Clothing, Furnishings, Boots, and Shoes. For many years various hotels occupied the second floor. One of the more unusual businesses to occupy the first floor was the Anti-Trust Fruit Store, named for the many antitrust suits brought against major corporations in the early 1900s. The building on Walnut Street houses a police station and other tenants today. (FCM H06185, *c.* 1926.)

THE COMMERCIAL BUILDINGS

First National Bank, College and Mountain Aves., Fort Collins, Colo.

The First National Bank, built in the early 1900s at the southeast corner of College and Mountain Avenues, graced downtown for six decades until it was demolished in 1961. Begun by pioneer settler Franklin Avery, the bank occupied several different spaces until moving into this marble and stone building. A more contemporary bank building stands at that corner today. (FCM H01454.)

Plays, musicals, and astounding performances by traveling entertainers brought in the crowds after the opera house was constructed at 121–127 North College Avenue. It was built in 1879 by a consortium of businessmen seeking to attract new residents by bringing culture to the town. William Jennings Bryan spoke there, and masquerade balls were held. The structure continued as an entertainment venue until the advent of motion pictures. Today it houses stores and offices; a farmer's and crafts market takes place in the winter months. (FCM H15877.)

THE COMMERCIAL BUILDINGS

In the frontier days, people relied on newspapers for news of events, news of their neighbors, and for an unfettered political slant. Ansel Watrous (second from right) came here in 1877; two years later his "Democratic" newspaper, the *Courier*, was a going concern, with the motto "home first; the world afterward." The newspaper eventually became the *Express Courier* in a different location. Today 243 Jefferson Street, where this photograph was taken, houses a yoga shop in a different building. (FCM H05309, *c.* 1884.)

The address 215 South College Avenue once belonged to the elegant home of the Benjamin Hottel family. Hottel, a cattleman and businessman, built the sizable stone house in 1883. Unable to withstand the transformation of College Avenue into a business district, it fell to the wrecking ball in 1962 to make way for a J. C. Penney store. Today the site is occupied by a hardware store. (FCM H03716, *c.* 1894.)

Featuring a turret and castellated Victorian styling, this gracious house, located at 202 Remington Street, was built by Charles Andrews with architect Montezuma Fuller in 1889. Dr. Peter McHugh bought it a few years later, converting the carriage house to the east into a private hospital described by a local newspaper as "a place to get well instead of to die." (See page 86.) One later occupant was the YWCA. Restored in 1977 and listed on the National Register of Historic Places, it survived by becoming a commercial business. (FCM H05809.)

Ranch-Way Feeds, 546 Willow Street, is the oldest continuing Fort Collins business still in the same location. Henry Clay Peterson and Elizabeth Stone opened the first mill on this site in 1869. B. F. Hottel later bought the flour mill. The Lindell mill survived multiple fires, one probably set by arsonists, and was rebuilt, expanded, and modernized each time. Today remnants of the earlier mill still survive in the current establishment, which supplies feed for large and small animals. (FCM H04533, c. 1900.)

THE COMMERCIAL BUILDINGS

CHAPTER 3

THE HOTELS

After passenger rail service came through town in 1877, the number of hotels downtown proliferated. One of the early hotels in Fort Collins was the Commercial, built by transplanted Englishman David Harris in 1879. By the beginning of the 20th century, portions of the structure had been moved to the triangular corner at College Avenue and Walnut Street. (FCM H09728, c. 1883.)

In 1904, a consortium of businessmen bought the Commercial Hotel, invested approximately $100,000, and opened it as the Northern Hotel. The first rendition of the hotel, with three floors, is shown above. Shown below is the hotel after a fourth floor was added. The hotel exterior featured a balcony over the entrance and a brick facade. (above, MEM, *c.* 1905; below, MEM, *c.* 1920.)

In 1936, the hotel underwent another remodel to achieve an art deco appearance. The brick exterior was stuccoed over; the lobby, with its distinctive staircase, was updated to the look of the times. A fire destroyed the upper two floors of the building in 1975, rendering the hotel uninhabitable, and it deteriorated for a time. In 2001, the upper floors were converted to apartments, with retail space on the main floor. (MEM, *c.* 1940.)

The lobby of the Northern Hotel reflects its early-20th-century elegance. Newspapers called the hotel "the pearl of northern Colorado." For a time, during the hotel's declining years, it housed elderly people on limited incomes. Today it has been remodeled and again serves as low-income senior housing. The furniture is different, but the lobby still looks much as it did more than 100 years ago. (FCM H08076a.)

A fire in the winter of 1880 destroyed the Welch Block at the northwest corner of College and Mountain Avenues, killing two people. But Jacob Welch reconstructed a grand, three-story edifice (corner building) that housed the elegant Windsor Hotel on the upper floors. Another fire in June 1885 damaged Welch's building again, and the Windsor Hotel moved into the Opera House (also visible here) next door. Welch removed the third floor, leaving only retail and office space, as is the case today. (FCM H02173, c. 1881.)

Perhaps the first Fort Collins structure built as a hotel, the National Hotel opened around 1870 on the northwest corner of Jefferson and Linden Streets. It was renamed the Cottage Hotel around 1905. Two stories high and 50 feet across the front, it was owned and operated for a time by Elizabeth "Auntie" Stone, often called the "Founding Mother of Fort Collins." Bolivar (Bob) S. Tedmon bought the building in 1879 and moved it up Jefferson Street to make room for his hotel, Tedmon House. (FCM H14759, *c.* 1905.)

The Tedmon House opened on the northwest corner of Jefferson and Linden Streets on May 20, 1880, measuring 94 by 60 feet and three stories in height. The local newspaper called it "a structure of beauty and solidity . . . visible from every portion of the town and attracting the eye for miles around." The Tedmon served Fort Collins until 1910, when both it and the Cottage House were torn down to make room for the Union Pacific's new right-of-way. Now the Jefferson Street Park stands in their stead. (FCM H06613, c. 1900.)

The Collins House was the first stone structure in Fort Collins, built in 1871 on the south side of Jefferson Street, east of Linden Street. In 1889, the Collins House had five fires in a short period of time and was renovated and renamed the City Hotel. By 1922, it was being used as a rooming house for Mexican sugar beet workers. It was razed in 1946. A small parking lot has replaced the building. (FCM H07975, *c.* 1900.)

THE HOTELS

This 1880 view, looking west on Jefferson Street, shows the Collins House on the left and the Tedmon House on the right. The Jefferson and Linden Street intersection was the heart of Fort Collins. Over time, the center of downtown shifted south and west, and many buildings in this area fell into disrepair. (FCM H01507 c. 1885.)

The La Court Hotel, at 232 Pine Street, had many names before being taken over by the Briggs family in the 1930s. Here it is the Farmers Hotel—$1 a day to board, $5 a week. When her family lived in the hotel, Arlene Briggs Ahlbrandt recalls that during the Depression rooms still went for $1 a night, with the owners grateful for the income. Until the 1970s, when closing became unavoidable, Ahlbrandt provided low-cost housing to seniors. Today the building is used as retail space and apartments. (Nadine Gates, c. 1912.)

To the left of the La Court Hotel (shown after the name change) sits the smaller Blaine Hotel, built in 1911 by Isaac Harris. It held 10 guest rooms and is shown here in 1936. In a later incarnation, the Blaine became the Pine Street Tavern. During a renovation in the 1980s, workers turned up old bottles and marbles buried under the floor, which had been raised to the level of the street after it was paved. The building is currently retail space. (Arlene Ahlbrandt, 1936.)

Note the pole in the middle of the doorway. The story goes that its purpose was to prevent robbers from riding their horses into the building, which began as the Poudre Valley Bank in 1882—with one table, two chairs, and a borrowed safe. Upstairs were the Masonic lodge and the U.S. post office. Later 250 Walnut Street became the Linden Hotel (with the pole removed), and in 1984, the Linden Square Partnership purchased it. A collapsed wall during renovation injured one person. The erstwhile bank now houses retail and office space. (FCM H01523, *c.* 1908.)

THE HOTELS

The Armstrong Hotel opened on April 7, 1923, on the northwest corner of South College Avenue and Olive Street to serve the auto-tourists who were flooding westward as cars became cheaper and more reliable and roads more accessible. The Armstrong has had its ups and downs, but now, renovated and looking much like it did in 1923, it is a boutique hotel serving guests just as it did in its heyday. (FCM H20874, *c.* 1928.)

Armstrong Hotel - Fort Collins, Colo.

One of the interior architectural features of the Armstrong is this curved staircase. Completed sometime in the 1930s and shown in the upper photograph in its art deco period, the current renovation is timeless and classic. Along with several other downtown buildings, the Armstrong Hotel is on the National Register of Historic Places. (MEM, *c.* 1935.)

STAIRWAY—LOBBY
ARMSTRONG HOTEL,
FORT COLLINS, COLO.

THE HOTELS

THE CHURCHES

Churches were always important to Fort Collins. Andrew Carnegie granted funds for a library here because of its abundance of churches and absence of bars. One of the oldest churches in town, with its congregation dating from 1867, the Methodist Episcopal Church on the southeast corner of College Avenue at Olive Street was constructed in 1898. It was replaced by an office building in 1964. (MEM, *c.* 1905.)

The First Presbyterian Church, organized in 1872, constructed this building on the southwest corner of Remington and Olive Streets in 1877 for $7,500. It became a Lutheran church after the Presbyterians moved in 1914. During a period of rapid growth in Fort Collins, the church was torn down. (FCM H08925, *c.* 1910.)

THE CHURCHES

In 1914, First Presbyterian erected the church shown here at the northwest corner of College Avenue and Myrtle Street. This building served the congregation until 1976, when congregational growth warranted a replacement. The current church faces Myrtle Street; the congregation now owns almost an entire square block. (FCM H02901.)

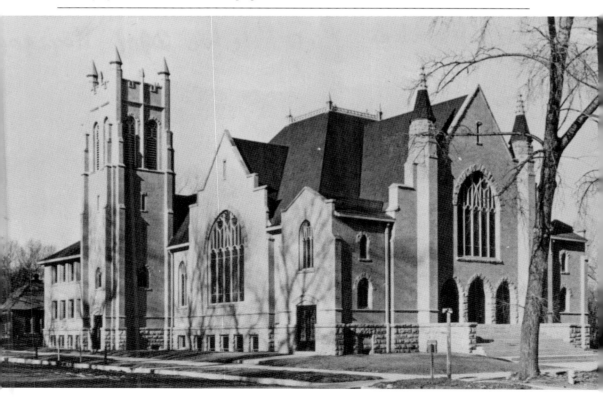

This elegant stone building at 300 West Mountain Avenue, Gothic in design but without the flying buttresses, has housed St. Joseph's Catholic Church since it was completed in 1901. The land was purchased from Franklin Avery. Remodeled in 1960, the church has never changed ownership or use. (FCM H02764, *c.* 1925.)

Around 1907, another Presbyterian congregation, First United Presbyterian, erected this small church on the southeast corner of Mathews and Mulberry Streets. In 1939, the American Lutheran Church, whose members wished to conduct services in English instead of the German preferred at Bethlehem Lutheran, purchased the property and did extensive remodeling; only the south wall of the building is original. When the congregation outgrew the space and relocated in 1974, Peak Community Church became the new and current owner. (FCM H15878, *c.* 1907.)

At the northeast corner of Olive and Howes Streets stood the Christian Science Church. The congregation, organized in 1897, met for a time in Unity Church until completing their own building. In the mid-1950s, the building was torn down, replaced by a parking lot. The congregation now has a newer home on West Mulberry Street. (FCM H00694, *c.* 1947.)

This lovely little building, at the southeast corner of College Avenue and Oak Street, served St. Luke's Episcopal Church's congregation from 1882 to 1965. It survived a windstorm during construction that collapsed the east wall and a fire in 1951 that destroyed a furniture store next door—parishioners wet down the roof for hours—but it could not survive progress. When the congregation outgrew it the church was demolished and the lot turned into commercial space, though some of the stained glass windows were saved. (MEM, *c.* 1920.)

The old brick church shown here was the first home of the First Baptist congregation, on the northeast corner of Remington and Magnolia Streets. Constructed in 1881, the little building soon proved inadequate as membership grew. In 1904, this structure was razed, replaced by the original version of the building shown below. Still used as a church, it has changed owners several times in recent years and underwent restoration and rehabilitation in the last decade, work which preserved the unique facade and rose window. (FCM H95283.)

THE CHURCHES

18 UNITY CHURCH FORT COLLINS COLO.

Built in 1905 for a congregation that began in 1898, Unity Church stood at the southwest corner of College and Mulberry Avenues. It was notable for hiring the first woman minister in Fort Collins, Mary Leggett. It became the Congregational Unitarian Church and served a small but influential membership, including college president Charles Lory, until 1968, when the congregation moved to a new home on Yorktown Avenue. The lot is now home to a fast food drive-through. (MEM, c. 1912.)

On May 1, 1898, the congregation of the First Christian Church dedicated their new building at the southeast corner of College Avenue and Magnolia Street. With a membership made up mostly of women, the minister, Rev. C. A. Wilson, contributed considerable work to the completion of the building. An art supply store has replaced the stately structure. (FCM H03690.)

Still standing at the southeast corner of Whedbee and Olive Streets is this stone church, once the home of Bethlehem Evangelical Lutheran, a congregation of German Russian immigrants drawn to the area by the sugar beet factory. Congregants dug the basement by hand, hauling stone from the nearby quarry by horse-drawn wagons. Reflecting the members' German heritage and new home in America, the cornerstone is carved in both English and German. Most recently occupied by an Episcopal congregation, the building was for sale as of 2010. (FCM H11921.)

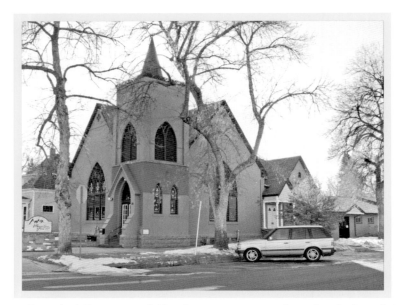

The German Evangelical Congregational Church, located at 201 Whedbee Street, was designed by prominent local architect Montezuma Fuller and was built in 1904. With a distinctive pressed-brick facade, the structure featured a 50-foot tower and circular seating in the sanctuary. In the 1940s, the congregation relocated and changed its name. Another owner, Bethel Baptist, built an addition. Most recently, the structure has served Mountain View Community Church, one of only a few surviving original churches in the downtown area still used for worship. (FCM H03664.)

THE CHURCHES

CHAPTER 5

THE COLLEGE AND THE SCHOOLS

The first classroom building on the Colorado State University campus, facing what is now College Avenue, was constructed in 1878. Old Main was all-purpose, with classrooms, offices, and living quarters for the college's first president. Around a century and several additions later, the rambling building was destroyed by fire, deliberately set during a period of student unrest in the 1970s. (MEM, *c.* 1895.)

Spruce Hall, now the oldest building on the Colorado State University campus, was originally constructed to house students. Built in 1881, not long after the college's first class of five graduated, it is sited on the land first plowed and planted to ensure establishment of an agricultural college in Fort Collins at the northeast corner of the campus. It is still in use. (MEM, *c.* 1910.)

The industrial sciences building began life in the 1880s as the mechanical arts building, where engineers would hone the skills they needed for a career in construction. Recently upgraded and renovated, the building, which faces onto Laurel Street, is at the northern edge of the now-sprawling campus. (MEM, *c.* 1912.)

15 C. A. COLLEGE MECHANICAL ENGINEERING BLDG. FORT COLLINS COLO.

Originally named the Botanical and Horticultural Laboratory, this brick building, in the folk Victorian cottage style, was constructed in 1890 north of Spruce Hall. It is now on the National Register of Historic Places. Through various name changes and uses, including several decades as the music conservatory, it has been in use by the college. Known today as Routt Hall, it houses administrative offices. (MEM, *c.* 1914.)

4833A   Old Domestic Science Hall, Ft. Collins, Colo.

Before Remington School was constructed in 1879, classes were held in a wooden building on Riverside Drive and in vacant storefronts. As the town grew, the need for a sizable school became apparent. The sturdy, square, brick structure at 318 Remington Street featured gaslights and central heating and had three teachers. It was razed in the 1970s to make room for the DMA Plaza senior housing. (FCM H02957.)

Only a few years after Remington School was built, the need for another school became clear. Franklin School, on the southwest corner of Mountain Avenue and Howes Street, was completed in 1887 for third- through eighth-grade students. On the upper floor, the district's first high school—an experiment—began in two classrooms. Four girls and one boy graduated in 1891. In 1959, Franklin School gave way to progress, replaced by a grocery store that was demolished in 2010. (FCM H02958.)

High school enrollment soon justified a separate building. The center section of Fort Collins High School, located at 417 South Meldrum Street, was designed by Montezuma Fuller on the classical model. It was completed in 1903. Boys entered on the south and girls on the north, with each having a separate lunchroom. Soon wings were added on either end. Upon completion of a new high school, this building became Lincoln Junior High School. In 1977, parts of the original building were incorporated into the new Lincoln Center. (FCM H08034.)

Saved from the wrecking ball, Laurel Street School, located east of College Avenue, is now Centennial High School, with a 21st-century addition that doubled the size of the original structure. Another Montezuma Fuller design, it was built in 1906 and is now the oldest school still operated by the Poudre School District. (FCM H01956.)

THE COLLEGE AND THE SCHOOLS

George Washington School, built in 1919 at 233 South Shields Street, reflected an era of reforms in education, exemplifying a move from the school as a place for moral inspiration to the school as a place for rational learning and nurturing of the young. The craftsman-style architecture was a departure from the earlier box-like Quincy style used for decades. In recent years, the building housed the Lab School for Creative Learning. That school was relocated, and this building is for sale as of 2010. (FCM H15893, *c.* 1919.)

When the new high school was built at 1400 Remington Street in 1925, residents complained that it was too far out of town. Initially voters turned down a bond for the school, but A. H. Dunn led a spirited, and ultimately successful, campaign to change their minds. Used until the new Fort Collins High School on Timberline Road was built in 1995, it is now the Colorado State University Center for the Arts. (FCM H23017, *c.* 1926.)

A small school, measuring 20 by 30 feet, was constructed at the northwest corner of South Shields Street and Drake Road in 1881. Designed by Montezuma Fuller, Pleasant View School combined many architectural elements. Despite preservationists' vigorous efforts to save the school in the aftermath of school-district consolidation, it was demolished in the 1970s, replaced by a shopping center. The Delehoy family rescued the bell tower. (FCM H15523.)

East of town, Plummer School (named for the adventurous pioneer who donated the land) was built on the northwest corner of Vine Drive (called Sugar Factory Road at the time) and Timberline Road in 1882. It featured Italianate styling, including Roman numerals to designate the year. Hope Sykes, author of a book about Russian German immigrants who grew sugar beets, taught immigrant children there and lived across the street in a house that is still standing. Abandoned after school consolidation, the building was renovated in the 1970s and is now privately owned, rented as an event center. (FCM H03170.)

CHAPTER 6

THE MUNICIPAL BUILDINGS

Erected in 1887 on Mason Street between Mountain Avenue and Oak Street, this Larimer County Courthouse was the third for the county. Fort Collins became the county seat in 1868. In 1888, frontier justice was meted out when vigilantes swung James Howe, who had that very day slit his wife's throat, from a construction derrick in front of the courthouse. The county has subsequently built two replacement courthouses on the same site, most recently in the early 21st century. (MEM, c. 1887.)

Fort Collins residents love a parade, as many early photographs show. This *c.* 1891 photograph was taken on Walnut Street, then the center of city government. City hall was in the center building, with the small triangular roof facade. To the right of city hall was the firehouse, with the tall tower for drying hoses. Built in 1881, the firehouse was staffed until 1915 by vigorous volunteers who occasionally competed with teams from other towns. Although the center of town was shifting south, Walnut Street remained a busy commercial district, just as it is today in the downtown historic district. (FCM H01579, *c.* 1891.)

THE MUNICIPAL BUILDINGS

The sign over the door to the left of the firehouse on Walnut Street reads "Free Reading Room"; it was the beginning of a public library in Fort Collins. Before the 20th century, libraries were often available only to subscribers. The firehouse was constructed after many buildings were lost to flames that could be fought only with bucket brigades and canal water. Today, though the reading room building is gone, Old Firehouse Books sells books in the former firehouse building. (FCM H00188, 1882.)

The Carnegie Library on Mathews Street was built in 1904 with a grant from philanthropist Andrew Carnegie, who was impressed with the town's family-centered, alcohol-free environment. The basement auditorium, where recitals were often held, became the home of the city's archival collection some years after the new library was constructed east of the Carnegie building, on Peterson Street. The future of this building, now the Fort Collins Museum and Discovery Center, has not been determined by the city, but it has been designated a local landmark to be preserved. (MEM, *c.* 1911.)

Carnegie Library, Fort Collins, Colo.

The sturdy wooden table seen in this photograph is still in use in the Carnegie building. While the building was the Fort Collins Public Library, it was used decade after decade by library patrons. This early-20th-century photograph was taken before an expansion in 1939 doubled the size of the facility. In the 1970s, the Carnegie building became the Fort Collins Museum, housing artifacts from pioneer days in Fort Collins. Several pioneer cabins are on the grounds. (FCM H0351, *c.* 1917.)

One of the earliest hospitals in Fort Collins was started by Dr. P. J. McHugh in the carriage house of his residence at the southeast corner of Remington and Oak Streets (see page 41). Complete with operating room, it opened in early 1906 and was called the McHugh Hospital. A local newspaper called it "entirely new and modern and strictly sanitary. . . . one of the finest private hospitals in the West." (FCM H08856.)

This building, at 301 East Magnolia Street, was once a hospital. It was constructed in 1906 by the Fort Collins Hospital Association. The doctors caring for patients there pledged "equal rights to all and special privileges to none." The need for a hospital had become clear after a typhoid epidemic at the beginning of the 20th century. The structure now houses apartments. (MEM, *c.* 1915.)

CHAS. T. GILBERT

THE FORT COLLINS HOSPITAL, FORT COLLINS, COLO.

When streetcar service was first approved by voters, the original cars were cumbersome Interurbans, with a large cattle guard in front, as shown in this photograph at College and Mountain Avenues. They experienced several encounters with animals, people, and cars before being replaced in 1919 by the lighter Birneys. In 1913, when a widespread blizzard shut down the entire state, even the heavy Interurbans could not get through the deep snow. (MEM, *c.* 1910.)

THE MUNICIPAL BUILDINGS

At 330 North Howes Street sits the street railway carbarn, once home to the streetcars that took passengers around town until the 1950s. Erected in 1907, the building is now used for storage, and the Fort Collins Municipal Railway Society is restoring a Birney streetcar there. Car No. 21, restored by this organization a number of years ago, travels along Mountain Avenue in the summer season. (Hazel Graves, *c.* 1907.)

Built in 1907 at 324 East Mountain Avenue to house a unit of the Colorado National Guard, the Armory had a stable and a firing range in the basement. Prepared to handle riots, fire, or floods, "the boys are . . . ready to help if necessary," said Captain Riddell in a newspaper article. The building, measuring 50 by 100 feet, had a balcony and skylights; the auditorium could seat 1,200. Dances, boxing matches, and even an indoor baseball game happened there. After several incarnations and alterations, the Armory is now rehabilitated as an events center. (FCM H09102, c. 1907.)

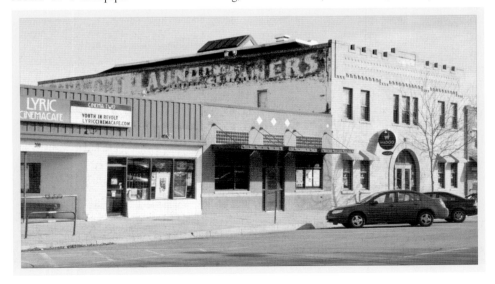

THE MUNICIPAL BUILDINGS

The Benevolent and Protective Order of Elks (BPOE) constructed this building at the northeast corner of Linden and Walnut Streets in 1903. Inside, a large stuffed elk stood next to a staircase. The Linden Hotel can be seen at left. The building remains, but at some point, the second floor was removed. A retail sporting-goods store occupies the space today. (MEM, *c.* 1912.)

Fort Collins has had a Masonic lodge since 1870. Here a large contingent of Masons assembles on Linden Street for a purpose lost to history. Sturdy footwear was needed in those days to cope with the unpaved streets, which could become mud-caked in rain and were the repository of horse droppings as well. As the companion photograph shows, many of the buildings are still standing. (FCM H07615, *c.* 1886.)

THE MUNICIPAL BUILDINGS

MASONIC TEMPLE FT COLLINS, COLO.

Constructed in 1925 by Fort Collins Masonic Lodge No. 19, the Masonic temple at the southeast corner of Oak and Howes Streets served a large membership, which had until then shared quarters belonging to other organizations. Still in use today by the Masons, it is now surrounded by office buildings, part of the bustling downtown scene. (MEM, *c.* 1953.)

MUNICIPAL TOURIST CAMP GROUND, CITY PARK, FT. COLLINS, COLO. N-286

As automobiles got cheaper and more reliable, and as improved roads were built, tourists flooded into the West. Many of the tourists were looking for low-cost lodging. Western towns, including Fort Collins, responded by building municipal campgrounds like this one, located in City Park and photographed in the 1930s. (MEM, *c.* 1930.)

THE MUNICIPAL BUILDINGS

During the 1920s and 1930s, City Park in west Fort Collins offered these cabins with carports as a step-up for the touring public. With a lake for swimming and fishing, a community house with showers and other modern conveniences, and affordable accommodations, the site drew travelers from all over the country. The cabins were dismantled during World War II, when gasoline became scarce. (MEM, *c.* 1930.)

TOURIST CABINS
CITY PARK - FT COLLINS COLO

DISCOVER THOUSANDS OF LOCAL HISTORY BOOKS FEATURING MILLIONS OF VINTAGE IMAGES

Arcadia Publishing, the leading local history publisher in the United States, is committed to making history accessible and meaningful through publishing books that celebrate and preserve the heritage of America's people and places.

Find more books like this at
www.arcadiapublishing.com

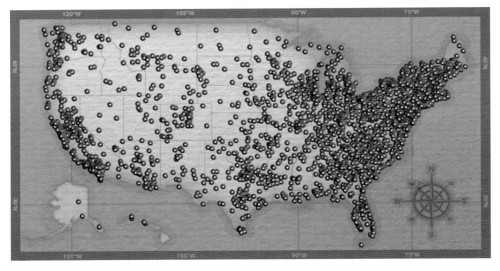

Search for your hometown history, your old stomping grounds, and even your favorite sports team.

Consistent with our mission to preserve history on a local level, this book was printed in South Carolina on American-made paper and manufactured entirely in the United States. Products carrying the accredited Forest Stewardship Council (FSC) label are printed on 100 percent FSC-certified paper.

MADE IN THE